Blissful
MOMENTS FOR WOMEN

Lovely Thoughts

on Everyday Life

BARBOUR

PUBLISHING

© 2012 by Barbour Publishing, Inc.

Print ISBN 978-1-61626-938-8

eBook Editions:
Adobe Digital Edition (.epub) 978-1-62029-622-6
Kindle and MobiPocket Edition (.prc) 978-1-62029-621-9

Devotional readings are from *365 Daily Whispers of Wisdom for Busy Women*, published by Barbour Publishing, Inc.

Prayers by Jackie M. Johnson are from *Power Prayers for Women*, published by Barbour Publishing, Inc.

Prayers by Donna K. Maltese are from *Power Prayers to Start Your Day*, published by Barbour Publishing, Inc.

Scripture quotations marked kjv are taken from the King James Version of the Bible.

Scripture quotations marked niv are taken from the HOLY BIBLE, NEW INTERNATIONAL VERSION®. niv®. Copyright © 1973, 1978, 1984, 2011 by Biblica, Inc.™ Used by permission. All rights reserved worldwide.

Scripture quotations marked nkjv are taken from the New King James Version®. Copyright © 1982 by Thomas Nelson, Inc. Used by permission. All rights reserved.

Scripture quotations marked nasb are taken from the New American Standard Bible, © 1960, 1962, 1963, 1968, 1971, 1972, 1973, 1975, 1977, 1995 by The Lockman Foundation. Used by permission.

Scripture quotations marked msg are from *THE MESSAGE*. Copyright © by Eugene H. Peterson 1993, 1994, 1995, 1996, 2000, 2001, 2002. Used by permission of NavPress Publishing Group.

Cover design by Kirk DouPonce, DogEared Design

Published by Barbour Publishing, Inc., P.O. Box 719, Uhrichsville, Ohio 44683, www.barbourbooks.com

Our mission is to publish and distribute inspirational products offering exceptional value and biblical encouragement to the masses.

 Member of the
Evangelical Christian
Publishers Association

Printed in China.

Contents

Introduction

Ahh, Bliss!

[Jesus] said. . . , "Come with me by yourselves
to a quiet place and get some rest."
MARK 6:31 NIV

No doubt about it, those much-longed-for
"ahh. . ." moments are few and far between. Take
a minute to revive and refresh your harried soul
with these bliss-filled scriptures, quotations, and
prayers that will invite you to rest and reflect
upon the everyday things that sweeten your life
and bring you a little closer to God.

Blessings

God can pour on the blessings
in astonishing ways.

2 CORINTHIANS 9:8 MSG

God Will Provide

Lord, I thank You for providing for my needs.

I give You my worries and fears—

those nagging thoughts about lacking money

for clothes, food, and the basics of life.

You feed the sparrows in the field, Lord—

You'll certainly help me and my family.

Your resources are limitless—

You have an abundance of blessings.

I praise You for Your goodness, Lord,

and the faithfulness of Your provision.

JACKIE M. JOHNSON

Give Thanks

Common courtesy grows more uncommon in our society with the passing of each generation. Finding someone who puts others first and uses words like *please* and *thank you* is like finding a rare gem. Most people hurry to their next task with little thought of others crossing their paths.

Every favor and earthly blessing that we experience is given to us by God. It is nothing we have accomplished in our own right. All that God has done since the beginning of creation, He did for humankind. You are His greatest treasure.

Give thanks to God today for giving you life—the very air you breathe. He has given you the ability to make a living, to feed your family, and to give to others. He is a good Father—He won't withhold anything good from you.

What has God done for you lately? What doors of opportunity has He opened? Give Him the credit, tell others of His goodness, and thank Him! It blesses God to hear you express your gratitude, and it will do your heart good as well.

SHANNA D. GREGOR

As God loveth a cheerful giver,
so He also loveth a cheerful taker. . .
who takes hold on His gifts
with a glad heart.

JOHN DONNE

"Give thanks to God. . . .
Shout to the nations, tell them what he's done,
spread the news of his great reputation!"

Living Well

Lord, when I think of "living well," help me to

be drawn toward Your ways, not the world's.

Show me the difference between what I want and

what I really need. Help me to know that my

true success lies in being right in love, wealthy in

good works toward others, and generous in sharing

from Your abundant blessing. I thank You for the

prosperity You provide, inside and out.

JACKIE M. JOHNSON

"The LORD bless you and keep you."

NUMBERS 6:24 NKJV

When we start to count flowers,
we cease to count weeds;
When we start to count blessings,
we cease to count needs;
When we start to count laughter,
we cease to count tears;
When we start to count memories,
we cease to count years.

Unknown

Whatever is true, whatever is noble,

whatever is right, whatever is pure,

whatever is lovely, whatever is admirable—

if anything is excellent or praiseworthy—

think about such things.

PHILLIPIANS 4:8 NIV

A Little Time with God

Susan headed out of her house in the same way she always did—in a hurry, guiding two children before her, double-checking their backpacks as she went, and reminding them of chores and practices scheduled for that afternoon. "Remember, 3:30 is ballet; 4:00 is soccer. I'll pick you up at school, but I have to go back to work, so—"

She stopped as her coat snagged on a bush. "What?—" She looked down to find her hem caught firmly by a cluster of thorns. As she stooped to untangle the cloth, the stem bent suddenly, and Susan found herself nose-to-petal with a rose. It smelled glorious, and she paused, laughing.

When Susan had planted the bush, a friend had asked why. "You never stop long enough to enjoy even what God drops in front of you. What makes you think you'll care about a rose?"

Susan glanced up toward the sky. "Thanks for grabbing me. I guess I should spend a little more time with You."

God blesses us every day in both great and simple ways. Children, friends, work, faith—all these things form a bountiful buffet of gifts, and caring for them isn't always enough. We need to spend a little time with the One who has granted us the blessings.

RAMONA RICHARDS

Boundless Grace

Lord, because of You, I have all I need.
You continually shower blessings upon me to the point
where they are overflowing. With Your support,
I can finally stand on my own two feet.
I even have enough left over to give to others and
to do the work that You have called me to do.
Thank You, Father, for blessing my life.

DONNA K. MALTESE

God's blessings are dispersed
according to the riches of His grace,
not according to the depth of our faith.

MAX LUCADO

Every good and perfect gift is from above,

coming down from the Father of the heavenly lights,

who does not change like shifting shadows.

JAMES 1:17 NIV

The Right Focus

Lord, I am thirsty, parched with the demands of this world. I am in want in so many ways. Help me not to focus on what I don't have, but to focus on You and the blessings that You have prepared for me and my children. Pour out Your Spirit upon me now. Fill me with Your presence. Give me hope for this day. I anticipate blessings waiting around every corner. Thank You, Lord, for taking such good care of me. You, my Savior, are the greatest blessing of all!

DONNA K. MALTESE

The Great Gift Giver

Do you know a true gift giver? We all give gifts on birthdays and at Christmas, when we receive wedding invitations, and when a baby is born. But do you know someone with a real knack for gift giving? She finds all sorts of excuses for giving gifts. She delights in it. A true gift giver has an ability to locate that "something special." When shopping for a gift, she examines many items before making her selection. She knows the interests and preferences, the tastes and favorites of her friends and family members. She chooses gifts they will like—gifts that suit them well.

God is a gift giver. He is, in fact, the Creator of all good gifts. He finds great joy in blessing you. The God who made you certainly knows you by name. He knows your tastes and preferences.

He even knows your favorites and your dreams. Most important, God knows your needs.

So in seasons of waiting in your life, rest assured that gifts chosen and presented to you by the hand of God will be worth the wait.

EMILY BIGGERS

Conversation

Be gracious in your speech. The goal is to bring

out the best in others in a conversation.

Reaching Out to Others

Lord, would You please show me how I can reach out to someone who needs a friend? Bring to mind people with whom I can share the love of Christ. Let my words and actions reflect Your love, acceptance, and compassion. Give me eyes to see the needs and a heart to respond. As I look out for the needs of others, and not just my own, I pray that I would be a vessel of Your blessing and joy.

JACKIE M. JOHNSON

Walk and Pray

Their friendship began when their daughters played on the same soccer team. Leaning against their cars, they chatted and waited for practice to end, both realizing after a couple of conversations that they had more in common than two energetic thirteen-year-old girls. They shared a common faith in God, and both women were experiencing the growing pains that come with parenting adolescents.

One day the women decided to start wearing their workout gear to practice so that they could talk and pray for their daughters as they walked the perimeter of the soccer field. By the end of the season, both women were encouraged and strengthened, and they had forged a deep friendship. The added bonus was their increased fitness levels derived from these long walks.

Jesus said, "For where two or three gather in my name, there am I with them" (Matthew 18:20 NIV). Real power is available when friends get together for fellowship and prayer, because Christ Himself is right there with them. Along with gaining another's insight and perspective, anytime we share a burden with a friend, our load instantly becomes lighter.

Is there a friend you might call today to join you in a prayer walk?

Austine Keller

The sweetest conversation between friends is the silent communication of their hearts.

BONNIE JENSEN

Watch the way you talk. . . .
Say only what helps, each word a gift.

EPHESIANS 4:29 MSG

Being a Better Listener

Lord, I praise You today for all You have done for me.

You have brought help, hope, healing, and restoration,

and I want to tell people! Help me proclaim Your

goodness, sharing the amazing ways You have come

through for me. But as I speak, help me to be a good

listener, too. Through Your Spirit, Lord, may I show

I care about my friends. Give me wisdom to know

when my ears should be open and my mouth shut.

JACKIE M. JOHNSON

Be thou an example of the believers, in word,

in conversation, in charity, in spirit, in faith, in purity.

*There are few things in life as
encouraging as the voice of a friend.
It's not just the words they speak,
but the gentle way they convey them.*

BONNIE JENSEN

May our Lord Jesus Christ. . .encourage your hearts

and strengthen you in every good deed and word.

2 THESSALONIANS 2:16–17 NIV

Well-Seasoned Speech

Cassie was a horrible cook! Her food was bland, flat, and boring to the extreme—no zest, no zing to tempt you for a second helping. Oh, she'd try to please people with what they wanted, but the result was pathetic.

As pale and uninviting as Cassie's food was, her conversations were the exact opposite: full of life, spiced with the hope of the gospel, meaty with truth, and sprinkled with kindness and love. People were drawn to her and would linger in conversation, savoring the sweet aroma of Christ that bubbled from within her. She didn't preach or use *Christianese*. Instead, she used words that encouraged, challenged, or piqued you for more. When asked about this, she admitted to making every effort to choose words that build up people, make them laugh, or give truths to chew on when they walk away–a practice of longer-lasting value than cuisine acclaim.

P. J. Lehman

Honoring Others with My Mouth

I don't need fancy words to impress others. I only need words guided by the mind of Christ. Help me, Lord, to honor others with my speech. I want to lift people up, not bring them down. I want to bring joy to the hearts of others, not sorrow. Give me a better attitude, positive words, and encouraging remarks. Guard my mouth and, when necessary, put Your hand upon it to keep it shut.

DONNA K. MALTESE

There is not in the world a kind of life
more sweet and delightful than that of
a continual conversation with God.

BROTHER LAWRENCE

Perfume and incense bring joy to the heart,

and the pleasantness of a friend springs

from their heartfelt advice.

PROVERBS 27:9 NIV

Building Blocks

Lord, I want to be a Barnabas—an encourager.
I want to build people up, block by block, and not
tear them down. Words can be so painful, so
wrenching to the soul, heart, spirit, and confidence of
others. Help me to be an encourager to others. Put a
kind word in my mouth. And as I do so, may others
continue to encourage me, especially those at church.
Sometimes, even there, we get our feelings hurt.
Help me to be Your representative, inside and
outside of the body of believers. Give me words
that are sweet to the soul!

DONNA K. MALTESE

Honest Friends

A woman clicked on an e-mail from one of her oldest and best friends. She had been thinking about this friend and had been meaning to call her, but it seemed life had just gotten in the way recently. She opened the e-mail thinking it would contain her friend's usual newsy musings about family, church, and the latest happenings. Instead, her friend made the stunning announcement that she believed their friendship had soured and she was wondering why. She explained that she hadn't received an e-mail, phone call, or a visit in months, and she wondered if she had done something—unwittingly—to offend her friend.

After the woman got over her shock, she began to feel defensive. "She's exaggerating. . .over-sensitive. . .completely wrong!" she cried. A little time and a lot of prayer revealed the truth—that she not only owed her friend an apology, but she would need to prove her worth as a friend once again.

God uses our relationships to make us better people, better Christians. An honest friend full of forgiveness and grace can open our eyes to our faults so we can then start making positive changes with God's help. The woman who admonished her friend was a true friend, and she valued the friendship so much that she was willing to risk rejection.

Does this kind of friend remind you of anyone?

Austine Keller

Family and Friends

She gets up while it is still night;

she provides food for her family. . . .

Her lamp does not go out at night.

PROVERBS 31:15, 18 NIV

Unconditional Love

Lord, I thank You for my family members and those who are like family to me. I am grateful for their love and understanding. May I be loving in return—not only with those who love me, but even with those who are hard to be around. Your ways are merciful and kind, forgiving and good. Help me to reflect Your love, finding joy in loving others as You love me.

JACKIE M. JOHNSON

Uniquely Wired

The Proverbs 31 woman puts Wonder Woman to shame. Up before dawn, late to bed, caring for her household, negotiating business contracts down at the city gate. . . She gives to the poor, plans for her household to run smoothly, anticipates future needs, such as snowy weather. Even her arms are buff! "She sets about her work vigorously; her arms are strong for her tasks" (Proverbs 31:17 NIV).

She is highly energetic, an efficiency expert, *and* gifted in relationships. "Her children arise and call her blessed; her husband also, and he praises her" (v. 28). This woman is downright intimidating!

So how do we benefit by reading about the Proverbs 31 woman? Reading about her day makes us feel overwhelmed, discouraged by our inadequacies. That bar is too high!

God doesn't place the bar so high that we live in its shadow. He wired each of us with different gifts, different energy levels, different responsibilities. Proverbs 31 casts a floodlight on *all* women—those gifted in business, in home life, as caregivers. This chapter displays how women undergird their families and their communities.

Remember, the book of Proverbs was written in the tenth century BC, when women were considered chattel. But not in God's eyes. He has always esteemed women and the many roles we fulfill in society.

suzanne woods Fisher

So much of what is great has sprung from the closeness of family ties.

JAMES M. BARRIE

I know that nothing is better for them than to rejoice, and to do good in their lives, and also that every man should eat and drink and enjoy the good of all his labor—it is the gift of God.

ECCLESIASTES 3:12-13 NKJV

Consistent Love

All I need is love! That's all I need from my friends right now. People who care about me, who want what's best for me, who will never turn away. But when I look at my past, I wonder if I've always loved my friends. I mean that constant, undying, unyielding love, the kind that You show for us. Forgive me, Lord, for the times I have fallen short. For times that I was so caught up in the busyness of my day that I did not show love to a friend who really needed it. Lord, fill me and my friends with Your love, and help us to let it flow freely to all we meet.

DONNA K. MALTESE

Greater love has no one than this,
than to lay down one's life for his friends.

The secret of a full and happy life is to wake up every morning with the intention of doing as much as we can to nurture the friendships God has given us. In no time at all the joy will begin to pour in. . . and our days will be filled with His goodness.

BONNIE JENSEN

Friends love through all kinds of weather,
and families stick together in all kinds of trouble.

PROVERBS 17:17 MSG

Practical Christian Advice

In 1 Peter 3:8, Peter intentionally lists godly traits in a particular order. First, live in harmony. In other words, get along. When we can live in peace with each other, we have already learned something about putting away our own selfishness. Second, be sympathetic. Sympathy implies that we feel sorry for those of our community in pain. Third, we must love as a family. Once we have begun to be sympathetic, natural love will spring up between us. Fourth, be compassionate. Compassion takes sympathy to the next level. We not only recognize hurt in our brothers and sisters and feel sorry for them from afar, but we long to relieve them of their burdens and pain. Finally, living together in harmony, being sympathetic and compassionate, and loving each other as brothers and sisters inevitably leads to humility. Humbling ourselves is putting aside our selfish natures and living for each other—the very thing Peter asks us to do.

When we embody these Christian attributes, imagine how we will revolutionize our relationships with our families, friends, coworkers, peers, and all those in between!

MANDY NYDEGGER

Thank You for My Friendships

Lord, I thank You for my wonderful friends! As I think about the treasure chest of my close friends, casual friends, and acquaintances, I am grateful for the blessings and the joys each one brings to my life. Thank You for my "heart" friends, my loyal sister friends who listen, care, and encourage me. They are my faithful companions. I acknowledge that You, Lord, are the giver of all good gifts, and I thank You for Your provision in my friendships.

JACKIE M. JOHNSON

*A person is made better
or worse by her friends.*

MABEL HALE

Finally, all of you, be like-minded, be sympathetic,
love one another, be compassionate and humble.

1 PETER 3:8 NIV

Blessed with Friends

There are many wonderful things in this life, Lord.
The smell of a baby's breath, the touch of a warm
hand, the taste of dark chocolate—but a good word,
deed, or thought from a friend is even better.
There are times when I am so down. And then a
friend blesses me and I think of You. It's because
of You and the love that You give that makes us
want to reach out to others. Thank You for blessing
my life with friends.

DONNA K. MALTESE

Be a Wise Builder

Every wise woman builds her house.

No matter the season of her life, no matter what house she is in, a woman should be about the business of building a home and a family.

An unmarried daughter can help build her father's house. A wife must build the home she and her husband have established. Even a widow can continue building her house for her children's children.

While home building is the highest calling of womanhood, we sometimes turn aside from it, thinking the world offers something better. We sometimes think the world's view of personal achievement is better than God's view of submission and self-sacrifice.

Don't be fooled—real wisdom is found as we

apply scripture to the many tasks of homemaking. Teaching kindness to a two-year-old is more difficult than teaching economic theory to graduate students. Clearly explaining salvation to a preschooler is more challenging than convincing a bank to finance a business plan.

When done well, home building will yield rewards for many generations. When done thoughtlessly, generations suffer.

Let's not neglect this great task for the Lord. Let us be wise builders.

HELEN W. MIDDLEBROOKE

God designed the family to be a spiritual garden that grows flowers for today and seeds for tomorrow.

DENNIS AND BARBARA RAINEY

For this reason I bow my knees to the Father of
our Lord Jesus Christ, from whom the whole
family in heaven and earth is named.

EPHESIANS 3:14–15 NKJV

Kindness and Love

Jesus answered and said to him,

"If anyone loves Me, he will keep My word;

and My Father will love him, and We will come

to him and make Our home with him."

The Reward

You promise me wonderful rewards when I am

charitable, Lord. I will be "like a watered garden,

and like a spring of water, whose waters fail not"

(Isaiah 58:11 KJV). Good health will come to me,

as well as good reputation, and I will live a life of

righteousness. Remind me of this the next time I

pass up a charity event for an evening in front of the

television set or hang up the telephone without even

listening to the caller. I cannot answer every request

made of me, so I count on You to guide me as to

where I should invest my efforts in such

as way as to bring You glory.

TONI SORTOR

Basic Math

If you disliked math in school, perhaps at some point you asked, *How will I ever use it in real life?*

A certain kind of relational math is fundamental to your daily life. The words and actions exchanged throughout your day add to or take away from your life and the lives of those around you. Are you a positive or negative force? Are those around you positive or negative influences in your life?

God's nature is to give—to add—to every life He encounters. As Christians, we are created in His image and should be positive influences on those around us each day. Look around you and determine who adds to your life and who takes away. You will probably find that you prefer to spend time with pleasant communicators. Words of anger, frustration, confusion, and jealousy take away from the spirit of a man, but words of affirmation and gestures of kindness add to every heart.

Think before you act. Consider your words before you speak. Will you be adding to that person or taking away with what you are about to say or do? Share the love God shows you with others.

shanna d. gregor

A kind heart is a fountain of gladness,
making everything in its vicinity
freshen into smiles.

washington irving

"Arise, shine, for your light has come,
*and the glory of the L*ORD *rises upon you."*

ISAIAH 60:1 NIV

Hospitality

Lord, I thank You for my home. Show my heart opportunities to open this home to others. I want to share what You've provided for me. As I practice hospitality, may Your love shine through my life. However my home compares with others', I thank You for what I have. I am grateful that Your Spirit is present here. Give me a generous, open heart, and use my home for Your good purposes.

JACKIE M. JOHNSON

She opens her mouth with wisdom,

and on her tongue is the law of kindness.

The nicest thing we can do
for our heavenly Father is to
be kind to one of His children.

st. teresa of avila

Be kind to one another, tender-hearted,

forgiving each other, just as God in Christ

also has forgiven you.

EPHESIANS 4:32 NASB

Reflections of Light

God said, "Light, be," and light came into existence. Light appeared from the lips of God so He could see all He was about to create–and His creation could see Him.

When you gave your heart to God, His light came on inside your heart. Christianity lives from the inside out. When your heart is right, then your actions truly portray the influence that God and His Word have in your life.

Your life should then begin to reflect the character and nature of the One who created you and to oppose all darkness. You are a reflection of His light to everyone around you. From within, you shine on the lives of others around you and become a light to the world.

As you point others to God, to His light–His

goodness, mercy, and love—your light shines, re-pelling darkness and giving comfort to everyone God brings across your path.

How encouraging to know your life can brighten the whole room. You have the power to open the door of people's hearts for the Holy Spirit to speak to them about their own salva-tion. Don't miss a moment to let your life shine!

shanna d. gregor

Praise for the Father of Compassion

Lord, You love us so much. Fill me with that love to overflowing. Give me a compassionate heart. Lead me to the concern You would like me to champion for You, whether it be working in a soup kitchen, helping the homeless, or adopting a missionary couple. Lead me in prayer as I go down on my knees and intercede for others in distress.

DONNA K. MALTESE

By showing love through acts of kindness,
we can point people toward the God
who is both kindness and love.

AMY NAPPA

But the fruit of the Spirit is love, joy,
peace, patience, kindness, goodness,
faithfulness, gentleness, self-control;
against such things there is no law.

GALATIANS 5:22–23 NASB

Compassion

Lord, Your compassion for people is great.
You healed the blind and You led the people who were
lost like sheep without a shepherd. Create in me
a heart of compassion—enlarge my vision so I see
and help the poor, the sick, the people who don't
know You, and the people whose concerns You lay
upon my heart. Help me never to be so busy or
self-absorbed that I overlook my family and friends
who may need my assistance.

JACKIE M. JOHNSON

Convenient Love

Christians have been given two assignments: Love God and love each other.

People say love is a decision. Sounds simple enough, right? The fact is that telling others we love them and showing that love are two very different realities. Let's face it—some people are harder to love than others. Even loving and serving God can seem easier on a less stressful day.

Think about convenience stores. They're everywhere. Why? Because along the journey people need things. It's nearly impossible to take a long road trip without stopping. Whether it's gas to fill our vehicles, a quick snack, or a drink to quench our thirst, everyone needs something. Gas station owners realize this—and we should, too.

It may not always be convenient to love God

when the to-do list stretches on forever or when a friend asks us for a favor that takes more time than we want to give. But God's love is available 24/7. He never puts us on hold or doles out love in rationed amounts. He never takes a day off, and His love is plentiful.

kate e. schmelzer

Laughter

and Joy

And Sarah said, "God has made me laugh,
and all who hear will laugh with me."

GENESIS 21:6 NKJV

Joy

Lord, You are my joy. Knowing You gives me gladness
and strength. As my heart's shield, You protect and
keep me from harm. Help me to face the future with
joy. Fill me with Your good pleasures so I may bring
enjoyment to my surroundings—at home, at work,
and in my ministry. Help me to laugh more and
smile often as I reflect on Your goodness.
In Your presence, Lord, is fullness of joy.

JACKIE M. JOHNSON

Contagious Laughter

Nothing brings more joy to our hearts than when God blesses our lives. Like Sarah, we may at first laugh with disbelief when God promises us our heart's desire. For some reason, we doubt that He can do what we deem impossible. Yet God asks us, as He did Sarah, "Is any thing too hard for the LORD?" (Genesis 18:14 KJV).

Then when the blessings shower down upon us, we overflow with joy. Everything seems bright and right with the world. With God, the impossible has become a reality. We bubble over with laughter, and when we laugh, the world laughs with us! It's contagious!

When Satan bombards us with lies—"God's not real"; "You'll never get that job"; "Mr. Right? He'll never come along"—it's time to look back at God's Word and remember Sarah. Embed in your mind the truth that with God, nothing is impossible (see Matthew 19:26). And then, in the midst of the storm, in the darkness of night, in the crux of the trial, laugh, letting the joy of God's truth be your strength.

DONNA K. MALTESE

It is pleasing to God whenever you rejoice or laugh from the bottom of your heart.

MARTIN LUTHER

Though you have not seen [Jesus], you love him;
and even though you do not see him now, you believe
in him and are filled with an inexpressible and
glorious joy, for you are receiving the end result
of your faith, the salvation of your souls.

1 PETER 1:8-9 NIV

Joyful in Hope

Lord, I thank You for giving me hope. I don't know
where I would be without You. I don't know what the
future holds, but You give me the ability to be joyful
even while I wait—even when I don't understand.
Please help me to have a positive attitude and live
with a mind-set of patience and courage as You work
Your will in my life. Help me to remain faithful in
prayer, Lord, and fully committed to You.

JACKIE M. JOHNSON

He will yet fill your mouth with laughing,

and your lips with rejoicing.

JOB 8:21 NKJV

Cheerfulness is the habit of looking at the good side of things.

W. B. Ullathorne

My heart leaps for joy,
and with my song I praise him.

Joy Is Jesus

As children, we find joy in the smallest things: a rose in bloom, a ladybug at rest, the circles a pebble makes when dropped in water. Then somewhere between pigtails and pantyhose our joy wanes and eventually evaporates in the desert of difficulties.

But when we find Jesus, "all things become new" as the Bible promises, and once again, we view the world through a child's eyes. Excitedly, we experience the "inexpressible and glorious joy" that salvation brings.

We learn that God's joy isn't based on our circumstances; rather, its roots begin with the seed of God's Word planted in our hearts. Suddenly, our hearts spill over with joy, knowing that God loves and forgives us and that He is in complete control of our lives. We have joy because we know this world is not our permanent home, and a mansion awaits us in glory.

Joy comes as a result of whom we trust, not in what we have. Joy is Jesus.

TINA KRAUSE

The Good Words

You have filled my mouth with laughter! My tongue is singing Your praises! I am so alive in You this morning. And it is because I am not only praying and reading Your Word, but I am allowing You to live in me and am putting Your Word into action. It can't get any better than this, and it's all because of Your sacrifice, Your dying for me. Thank You, Jesus, for making me whole and happy in You!

DONNA K. MALTESE

For those who love God,
laughter isn't optional, it's scriptural.

LIZ CURTIS HIGGS

"Do not grieve, for the joy

*of the L*ORD *is your strength."*

NEHEMIAH 8:10 NIV

I Need More Joy

Lord, buoy my spirits. I need more joy in my life. Daily living and trials can be so depleting; I just can't do it on my own. Help me to laugh more and enjoy life again. Help me to have a childlike, playful spirit—a lighter heart, Lord. Encourage me so I can bless others with a kind word or a smile. Let me come to Your dwelling place and find strength and joy in praising You. In Your presence is fullness of joy!

JACKIE M. JOHNSON

Made to Laugh

Comedians live their lives to make people laugh. From famous actors on the movie screen to the class clown at a local high school, we take a moment to celebrate with them. Sometimes the many worries in life keep us from letting our guard down, relaxing and enjoying the little things in life that bring us great joy and laughter.

It feels good to laugh—from a small giggle that you keep to yourself to a great big belly laugh. It is a wonderful stress reliever or tension breaker. How many times have you been in an awkward situation or in a stressful position and laughter erupted? It breaks the tension and sets our hearts and minds at ease.

As children of the Creator Himself, we were made to laugh—to experience great joy. Our design didn't include for us to carry the stress, worry, and heaviness every day. When was the last time you really had a good laugh? Have you laughed so hard that tears rolled down your cheeks? Go ahead! Have a good time! Ask God to give you a really good laugh today.

shanna d. gregor

Nature

And seeing the multitudes, he went up into a mountain: and. . .his disciples came unto him: and he opened his mouth, and taught them.

MATTHEW 5:1–2 KJV

A World in One Drop

O Lord, I have peered into a microscope and seen a world in one drop of water. I have gazed through a telescope and have seen stars and galaxies uncountable. When I see the majesty of Your vast creation, I am brought to my knees in wonder.

But in my humble admiration, there is also a desperate question: Do You notice me and concern Yourself with me? I thank You, Lord, for personally answering my question. When I am apprehensive, I put my trust in You, and You keep me safe. When I am lonely, You talk to me. When I am sad, You make me happy. When I am weak, I bow before You and feel Your strength.

JOHN HUDSON TINER

God's Mountain Sanctuary

Melissa felt crushed beneath work, home, and church responsibilities. So much so, she could no longer give or listen, let alone hear from God. So she decided to take a day trip to the mountains to try and unwind.

There the forest hummed with a symphony of sound as beams of sunlight filtered through the vast timberland. As she strolled a wooded path, she noticed how God's creation kept perfect cadence with its Creator. No one directed the wildflowers to bloom, no one commanded the trees to reach upward, and no one forced the creek to flow downstream. No one but God, and nature simply complied.

Jesus often retreated to a mountain to pray. There He called His disciples to depart from the multitudes so that He could teach them valuable truths—the lessons we learn from nature. Don't fret: Obey God's gentle promptings, and simply flow in the path He clears.

Do you yearn for a place where problems evaporate like the morning dew? Do you need a place of solace? God is wherever you are—behind a bedroom door, nestled alongside you in your favorite chair, or even standing at a sink full of dirty dishes. Come apart and enter God's mountain sanctuary.

TINA KRAUSE

All things bright and beautiful,
All creatures great and small,
All things wise and wonderful,
Our Lord God made them all.

cecil Frances Alexander

"You will go out in joy and be led forth in peace;
the mountains and hills will burst into song before you,
and all the trees of the field will clap their hands."

ISAIAH 55:12 NIV

A Special Planet

Heavenly Father, the photographs of Earth taken
from space always cause me to pause because of
the stunning beauty they reveal: green forests,
brown deserts, white clouds, and blue-green oceans.
The earth looks like a marvelous jewel set against
the black background of space. It causes me to adore
You, Lord, and remember You as the Creator.
Father, I appreciate the earth as Your special
creation. Keep me alert to the goodness around me.
But help me always be mindful that this earth is not
my permanent home. Despite its beauty, the earth is
but a way station to a much grander place with You.
May I always live my life with the knowledge that
heaven is my eventual destination.

JOHN HUDSON TINER

The grass withers, the flower fades,

but the word of our God stands forever.

For in the true nature of things,
if we will rightly consider, every green
tree is far more glorious than if it
were made of gold and silver.

MARTIN LUTHER

"If God gives such attention to the appearance of wildflowers—most of which are never even seen—don't you think he'll attend to you, take pride in you, do his best for you?"

MATTHEW 6:30 MSG

Created vs. Creator

The sun, moon, and stars are not to guide our lives, regardless of the power their light seems to have over us or the horoscopes people have concocted. God placed those lights in the sky with the touch of His little finger and could turn them off again, if He so chose, with less effort than it would take to flip a switch. They are beautiful creations, but they do not compare with the Creator!

Once in a while nature takes our breath away. We marvel at snowcapped mountains or get caught up in the colors of a sunset. Our heavenly Father is like a loving parent on Christmas Eve who arranges gifts beneath the tree, anticipating the joy those gifts will bring to his children.

When God fills the sky with a gorgeous sunset, it is not just about the colors and the beauty. Those colors reflect His love. He paints each stroke, each tiny detail, and mixes purples with pinks and yellows so that you might *look up*! When you look up to find the bright lights that govern our days and nights, or the next time you see a sunset, remember the Creator and give Him glory.

EMILY BIGGERS

Living Daily with Delight

Lord, I thank You for the joy You bring every day.
Whether I go out or stay in, joy is with me—because
You are there. Lead me forth today in peace.
May all creation—even the trees of the field—praise
You as I as praise You. Help me to live with a lighter
heart and a positive attitude despite the distractions
and duties that seek to steal my joy. I choose You.
Help me to live daily with Your delight.

JACKIE M. JOHNSON

The course of Nature is the art of God.

EDWARD YOUNG

"And when you look up to the sky and see the sun, the moon and the stars—all the heavenly array—do not be enticed into bowing down to them and worshiping things the LORD your God has apportioned to all the nations under heaven."

DEUTERONOMY 4:19 NIV

Hope in God,
Rich in Generosity

I am setting my hope on You this morning,

Lord, for You provide me with everything to enjoy.

Your treasure of creation—trees, flowers, children,

animals, sunsets, stars—are wonders to my eyes and

a balm to my heart. With You supplying all that

I need, I can do good works, be ready to share,

and thus build up treasures in heaven. This way of

life, enveloped by Your presence, is the true way.

Keep my feet sure on this path. Take care of me

today and through the days to come.

DONNA K. MALTESE

Nature Rejoices

The bumblebee yellow float plane dropped off the young couple and their guide near a remote lake in the wilds of Alaska. It was their first Alaskan adventure vacation, and they expected to catch a lot of fish, but they hadn't realized how awestruck they would be as they drank in the majestic views that surrounded them. Standing in thigh-deep glacial waters, they cast their lines. A snowcapped volcano rose up on their left, and an ancient glacier reflected the sun on their right. The only sounds were those of nature itself—the rushing river, the wind in the trees, and an occasional whoop from the woman when she got a fish on her hook. They marveled at the pair of bald eagles that soared above them most of the day and the young bear that came out of the bush to investigate the strangers who had usurped his fishing rights.

We don't have to be outdoorsmen like our Alaska vacationers to appreciate and be inspired by the wonders of God's creation wherever we find ourselves. Wildflowers that grow alongside highways, a shed snakeskin—a found treasure that a boy brings to his mother—or the unusual cloud formations that dance in the sky before a storm inspire us to praise God, the Creator of all things. Nature declares the glory of the Lord.

Austine Keller

Natural laws were created by
Christ and they alter at His bidding.

JOHN PIPER

Thou art my hiding place.

PSALM 32:7 KJV

Prayer

I call on you, my God, for you will answer me;

turn your ear to me and hear my prayer.

PSALM 17:6 NIV

The Delight of Answered Prayer

Lord, I thank You for the joy of answered prayer!

You are amazing. I delight in You and thank You with

a full heart. I asked and You answered. I receive what

You give with a grateful heart. Lord, You are good.

You are faithful. You are my joy and my delight.

I praise Your holy name. I am smiling at You right now.

Thank You for filling my heart with gladness, Lord.

JACKIE M. JOHNSON

Available 24/7

No one is available to take your call at this time,
so leave a message and we will return your call—
or not—if we feel like it. . .and only between the
hours of 4:00 and 4:30 p.m. Thank you for call-
ing. Have a super day!

We've all felt the frustration of that black
hole called voice mail. It is rare to reach a real,
honest-to-goodness, breathing human being the
first time we dial a telephone number.

Fortunately, our God is always available. He
can be reached at any hour of the day or night
and every day of the year—including weekends
and holidays! When we pray, we don't have to
worry about disconnections, hang-ups, or poor
reception. We will never be put on hold or our
prayers diverted to another department. The

Bible assures us that God is eager to hear our petitions and that He welcomes our prayers of thanksgiving. The psalmist David wrote of God's response to those who put their trust in Him: "He will call on me, and I will answer him" (Psalm 91:15 NIV). David had great confidence that God would hear his prayers. And we can, too!

Austine Keller

You pay God a compliment by asking great things of Him.

st. teresa of avila

Why, my soul, are you downcast?

Why so disturbed within me? Put your hope in God,

for I will yet praise him, my Savior and my God.

PSALM 42:11 NIV

Rewards of Belief

From the beginning of time, Lord, You have been the One. You are the Ancient of Days. I humbly come before You, earnestly seeking Your face. I am awed by Your presence and staggered by Your might and power. Hear my prayer, O Lord. Reward me with Your peace and Your strength. I believe in You.

DONNA K. MALTESE

Let my prayer be set before You as incense,

the lifting up of my hands as the evening sacrifice.

PSALM 141:2 NKJV

We do not need to search for heaven over here or over there in order to find our eternal Father. In fact, we do not even need to speak out loud, for though we speak in the smallest whisper or the most fleeting thought, He is close enough to hear us.

st. teresa of avila

In the morning, L<small>ORD</small>, you hear my voice;

in the morning I lay my requests

before you and wait expectantly.

<small>PSALM</small> 5:3 <small>NIV</small>

Yet Praise Him

Many individuals and prayer groups use the acronym ACTS to guide their prayers. The letters stand for Adoration, Confession, Thanksgiving, and Supplication. Note that adoration comes first, before the believer confesses sin, thanks God, or asks anything of Him. God delights in His children's praise and adoration.

If you have cared for a child, you have probably received genuine adoration at times as well as times of appreciation in response to something you have done for her or him. Which warms your heart more? Certainly it means more to be held in high esteem simply because of who you are in the child's life than to be told "I love you" when you hand out dollar bills or promise a trip to the zoo!

Imagine how God feels when one of His children praises Him simply for who He is, even when her circumstances are far from perfect. Don't you suppose it feels like a tight hug around His neck? A "just because" sort of hug, not the "I got something from you" sort.

Praise God regardless. Praise Him yet, as the psalmist did. Adore Him today, for He is God.

EMILY BIGGERS

In His Time

Lord, sometimes I don't understand why it takes
so long for You to answer some of my prayers.
At times Your answers are immediate, but on other
occasions, I need to keep coming before You,
asking over and over again for You to meet my need.
Help me to grow during this time, Lord. Give me the
confidence to ask and keep on asking.

DONNA K. MALTESE

Sometimes a person prays with his tears,
even when words are missing.

BILL GOTHARD

Epaphras. . .a servant of Christ Jesus. . .is always wrestling in prayer for you, that you may stand firm in all the will of God, mature and fully assured.

COLOSSIANS 4:12 NIV

Joy in Praying for Others

Lord, I thank You for the joy and privilege of praying for others. What a blessing to be able to intercede, to stand in the gap and move heaven and earth for those I love. In all my prayers for those I know, may I have a heart of joy. Bless my family and friends, Lord. Bless those who need You today. May I find satisfaction in lifting up prayers for others.

JACKIE M. JOHNSON

Be Still

From the minute the alarm clock goes off in the morning, we are busy. Many women rush off to work or begin their tasks around the house without even eating breakfast. Most of us keep hectic schedules, and it is easy to let the day pass by without a moment of peace and quiet.

In Psalm 46:10 the command to *be still* is coupled with the result of *knowing that He is God.* Could it be that in order to truly recognize God's presence in our lives, we must make time to quiet ourselves before Him?

Sitting quietly before the Lord is a discipline that requires practice. Just as in our earthly relationships, learning to be a good listener as we converse with our heavenly Father is important.

If prayer remains one-sided, we will miss out on what He has to say to us.

Although God may not speak to us in an audible voice, He will direct our thinking and speak to our hearts. Stillness allows us to dwell on God's sovereignty, His goodness, and His deep love for us. He wants us to remember that He is God and that He is in control, regardless of our circumstances.

Be still. . .and know that He is God.

EMILY BIGGERS

Rest and Relaxation

A twinkle in the eye means joy in the heart,
and good news makes you feel fit as a fiddle.

PROVERBS 15:30 MSG

No Need to Count Sheep

There are times, Lord, when I climb into bed, shut my eyes, and fall right to sleep. I wake up the next morning refreshed. There are other times, Lord, when the events of the day, the week, the month, follow me to bed and I lay there in turmoil. Lord, with You as my friend, how can I worry about my enemies? You constantly watch over me.

pamela kaye tracy

How About Some Fun?

"Have you had any fun this week?"

This query, in and of itself, might sound odd, but two friends agreed to ask each other this question periodically because both had the tendency to plow through an entire week of school, work, church, and community commitments forgetting—or neglecting—to plan an activity or two for the sole purpose of recharging their own burnt-out batteries. Both women realized they would have to make an effort to carve out time for activities that brought them joy. For one, it was kayaking and hiking; for the other, it was settling into her favorite reading chair with a mystery novel.

God does not want His kids to be worn out and stressed out. He did not design us to be like little Energizer Bunnies that keep on going and going and going. We need time to *recreate*–to revive and refresh our bodies and minds. A little relaxation, recreation–and yes, *fun*–are essential components of a balanced life. Even Jesus and His disciples found it necessary to get away from the crowds and pressures of ministry to rest.

There's a lot of fun to be had out there–playing tennis or golf; jogging; swimming; painting; knitting; playing a musical instrument; visiting an art gallery; playing a board game; or going to a movie, a play, or a football game. Have you had any fun this week?

Austine Keller

Relaxation was God's idea.

GINA MASELLI

I pray that God, the source of hope, will fill you completely with joy and peace because you trust in him. Then you will overflow with confident hope through the power of the Holy Spirit.

ROMANS 15:13 NLT

Spiritual Health

Lord, I need Your times of refreshing in my life.

Bread of Heaven, as You nourish my body with

food, feed my soul with Your words of comfort

and life. May I be filled with Your healing love,

joy, and goodness. I praise You, Father, for providing

green pastures, places to relax and unwind in the

Spirit. Please still my heart from distractions

and be the restorer of my soul.

JACKIE M. JOHNSON

Return to your rest, O my soul,

for the Lord has dealt bountifully with you.

PSALM 116:7 NKJV

Take rest; a field that has
rested gives a bountiful crop.

o v i d

Relax, everything's going to be all right;

rest, everything's coming together;

open your hearts, love is on the way!

JUDE 1 MSG

God of Hope

In our busy, fast-paced lives, we may feel exhausted at times. Our culture fosters frenzy and ignores the need for rest and restoration. Constantly putting out fires and completing tasks, working incessantly, we may feel discouraged and disheartened with life. There is more to life than this, isn't there?

Our God of hope says, "*Yes!*" God desires to fill us to the brim with joy and peace. But to receive this gladness, rest, and tranquillity, we need to have faith in the God who is trustworthy and who says, "Anything is possible if a person believes" (Mark 9:23 NLT). We need to place our confidence in God who, in His timing and through us, will complete that task, mend that relationship, or do whatever it is we need. The key to receiving and living a life of hope, joy, and peace is recounting God's faithfulness out loud, quietly in your heart, and to others. When you begin to feel discouraged, exhausted, and at the end of your rope, *stop*; go before the throne of grace and recall God's faithfulness.

TINA C. ELACQUA

Praise Ye the Lord

I praise God from whom all blessings flow. You bless us beyond measure, we the sheep of Your pasture. You give us green meadows in which to lie down, calm waters to give us rest. You forgive us our sins. You love us beyond measure. There is no greater blessing than Your presence in my life, than Your desire to hear of all my troubles, cares, and woes. You are here to lift the burden from my shoulders and shower blessings down upon me. I praise the name of Jesus in whom I cannot but trust.

DONNA K. MALTESE

*God's purposes may best be
accomplished through our inactivity.*

JANE RUBIETTA

Take my yoke upon you and learn from me,

for I am gentle and humble in heart,

and you will find rest for your souls.

Getting Rid of Stress

Lord, help me to find relief from stress in my life.
I need to value rest and make time to relax—and I
need Your power to do so. I cast my cares on You,
my burden bearer. Help me to deal with the toxic,
unhealthy relationships in my life. Give me the
strength to say no when I need better emotional
boundaries. And please help me find joy again in the
things I like to do—unwinding with music, taking a
walk, calling a friend, or learning a new hobby.
Calm me and renew me, Lord.

JACKIE M. JOHNSON

Margin

Imagine a busy person's planner or calendar. More often than not, it is bursting with notes and reminders and is well-worn from frequent use. Seldom is there an opening in the day's schedule for unexpected things that may arise, let alone a few minutes set aside for rest. But God instructs us to plan for rest in our schedule and to leave ourselves some breathing room in order to accommodate last-minute things.

Hebrews 4 refers to the final, eternal rest that we will enter into with Christ. But in the meantime, we are called to lead an uncluttered life so we are ready for service to God. We are not to busy ourselves with the cares of the world, completely filling our margins.

Does your life have a clean margin, or have

you filled your page completely, leaving no room for additions or corrections? Is there room in your life for the plans God has for you?

nicole o'Dell

Simple Pleasures

A happy heart makes the face cheerful.

PROVERBS 15:13 NIV

Faith and Wellness

Nine simple words—"Rise and go; your faith has made you well." What a treasure they are! Keep them in my mind and heart today. Help me to retain their sounds, meaning, and import. May I rise from this place of prayer full of faith that heals my mind, body, spirit, and soul. Thank You, Lord.

DONNA K. MALTESE

The Secret of Serendipity

Can you remember the last time you laughed in wild abandon? Better yet, when was the last time you did something fun, outrageous, or out of the ordinary? Perhaps it is an activity you haven't done since you were a child, like slip down a waterslide, strap on a pair of ice skates, or pitch a tent and camp overnight.

Women often become trapped in the cycle of routine, and soon we lose our spontaneity. Children, on the other hand, are innately spontaneous. Giggling, they splash barefoot in rain puddles. Wide-eyed, they watch a kite soar toward the treetops. They make silly faces without inhibition; they see animal shapes in rock formations. In essence, they possess the secret of serendipity.

A happy heart turns life's situations into opportunities for fun. For instance, if a storm snuffs out the electricity, light a candle and play games, tell stories, or just enjoy the quiet. When we seek innocent pleasures, we glean the benefits of a happy heart.

Jesus said, "I am come that they might have life, and that they might have it more abundantly" (John 10:10 KJV). God wants us to enjoy life, and when we do, it lightens our load and changes our countenance.

So try a bit of whimsy just for fun. And rediscover the secret of serendipity.

TINA KRAUSE

*Into all our lives, in many simple, familiar,
homely ways, God infuses this element of joy
from the surprises of life, which unexpectedly
brighten our days and fill our eyes with light.*

<small>HENRY WADSWORTH LONGFELLOW</small>

*For the earth is the L*ORD*'s,*

and all it contains..

1 CORINTHIANS 10:26 NASB

Finding Contentment

Lord, please help me to find my contentment in You. I don't want to be defined by "stuff"—the things I own or what I do. May my greatest happiness in life be knowing who You are and who I am in Christ. May I treasure the simple things in life, those things that bring me peace. With Your grace, I rest secure.

JACKIE M. JOHNSON

For our boasting is this: the testimony of our conscience that we conducted ourselves in the world in simplicity and godly sincerity, not with fleshly wisdom but by the grace of God.

2 CORINTHIANS 1:12 NKJV

Holy Comforter, fill my deepest longings with Your quenching presence. Keep me looking only to You for soul satisfaction. Amen.

P. J. Lehman

All my longings lie open before you, Lord;

my sighing is not hidden from you. . . .

My soul thirsts for God.

PSALM 38:9; 42:2 NIV

Comfort Food

A big mound of ice cream topped with hot fudge; a full bowl of salty, buttery popcorn; grilled cheese sandwiches and warm chicken noodle soup fixed by Mom—comfort food. There is nothing like a generous helping of things that bring the sensation of comfort to a worn body at the end of a long day or to a bruised mind after a disappointment. Those comfort foods soothe the body and mind because, through the senses, they remind us of happier and more secure times.

Romans 15:4 tells us that the scriptures are comfort food for the soul. They were written and given so that, through our learning, we would be comforted with the truths of God. Worldly pleasures bring a temporary comfort, but the problem still remains when the pleasure or comfort fades. However, the words of God are soothing and provide permanent hope and peace. Through God's Word, you will be changed, and your troubles will dim in the bright light of Christ. So the next time you are sad, lonely, or disappointed, before you turn to pizza, turn to the Word of God as your source of comfort.

NICOLE O'DELL

A New Mind

Lord, I seem to have the wrong mindset today.
Instead of looking to Your leading, I seem to be
focused in on the worldly aspects of life. And I know
that's not where You want my thoughts to be.
Give me the mind of Christ. Make my needs simple.
Change my life, my thoughts, my desires. I want to
live a life that is good, perfect, and pleasing to You.

DONNA K. MALTESE

Nothing makes a journey more difficult than a heavy backpack filled with nice but unnecessary things. Pilgrims travel light.

RANDY ALCORN

*The L**ORD** preserves the simple.*

PSALM 116:6 NKJV

Lead Me by the Hand

Here we go, Lord—another morning with a thousand things to do. Lead me by the hand, for I don't know which way to go. I have trouble with my priorities, Lord. The only thing I seem to be able to remember is that You are first in all things. So here I am, seeking You first. Plan my day as You see fit. Direct my steps to walk Your path. Life can get so complicated, Lord, so help me to keep it simple, remembering that You are working in me both to will and to do for Your pleasure.

DONNA K. MALTESE

Overwhelmed Is Underprayed

Live quietly, mind your own business, work hard, serve on the PTA, chair some committees, sign the kids up for soccer, join an aerobics class. . ." Oops! Is that what it says, or did we add something to the recommendations in the Bible?

None of these things are bad or wrong. However, moving through life as a tornado, leaving destruction in your wake, affects the lives of those around you. To be an effective witness for Christ, you must be in control of your affairs. To be able to attest to the comfort and peace that Jesus provides, you cannot be frantic and out of control.

If your mantra is "I'm overwhelmed," followed by a familiar litany of tasks, duties, and deadlines, perhaps you have not fully sought the

will of God regarding your schedule and commitments. His desire is not to overwhelm you.
He recommends that you do your very best to
lead a quiet, simple life while you work hard at
the things you need to do. Find peace as you
release yourself from self-imposed requirements
and surrender to God's will.

NICOLE O'DELL